Ways to Win at Writing... and Editing!

Chelsia McCoy

Published in the United States of America. Houston, Texas.

ISBN - 9798386262112

Request for information should be directed to:
support@yourwritingtable.com

Cover design by: Your Writing Table (www.yourwritingtable.com)

Dedication

For all the women who have a story to tell
and NOW you are ready to tell it.

Your words...
Your voice...
Your story...
Your experiences...
It all matters!

You CAN & WILL win at writing!

Table of Contents

Introduction

You have a story to tell and you're ready to write it. The book is in you. It's been in you. You have talked about it, dreamed about it, even wrote a date in your planner showing your "start" date. In between picking up the kids from school and ordering pizza for dinner, you're gonna start writing. The idea has been sitting in your mind for years and now... *now* you are really, really ready to take it from that idea to an actual book.

But how do you start? Like, really... How?

You have the ideas, but how do you actually get them from your brain to the paper in a way that will actually make sense to those who read it?

Wait – who's gonna read it?

What is the title going to be?

Is anyone gonna be interested in what you choose to write about because you know 50 million other women have written books about this same topic already, right?

How much is it gonna cost you? Wait... there's a cost?

And you admit you're not the *best* speller... you did alright in school, but writing a book is totally different. Not to mention life has been "life-ing" and writing a book never seems to get scratched off the "To Do" list or the daily, weekly and monthly planner.

Oh great. Now you don't know what the book cover will look like, either.

And let's not even talk about promoting and how people will know you even wrote a book.

And *then* your friend at church has already written four books and now she's working on her fifth. She said she was gonna help you, but that hasn't happened and if you watch one more YouTube video on "how to write a book," you're gonna scream.

There's no way you're gonna write a book. Nope.

And *then* you presented your story idea to an actual publishing company, and they rejected it... said your manuscript "wasn't the right fit" for them at this time.

Now, you've given up.

Or you're about to give up.

WAIT! There is hope!

I can relate to all of these scenarios because I have experienced all of them. Yep, I started and stopped… watched others write and publish multiple books but I had yet to follow through on my own ideas. My first book was a fictional novel that was completed in 2005. I started writing it about 10 years prior to that. And of course, LIFE happened. Graduated from high school, went to college, got married, had kids, divorced, relocated to another state and THEN completed the book somewhere in the mix of all that. Whewwww! in so many disorganized parts and tidbits. Literally, it was a page here, an idea there… I had no knowledge at that time on the correct way to write a book. I just went with the flow in my brain; or when I sat down long enough to jot something down.

Once that book was complete, I actually took the time to write the sequel. I had a bit more diligence and commitment to writing so before I knew it, I had completed another book in 9 months. That may seem like a long time to some of you, but for me, at that time (juggling being a single parent and working full time) that was awesome!

Some of you have experienced similar things. "Life" has happened and you don't know when you will have the time to write a book. Some of you have so much to tell but you don't know how. Some of you know you have a book you want to write, but you just aren't sure about "telling it all." Or some of you get hung up on the fact that you want to share, but you don't want to "put all your business in the street." I get it and I've been there. You know that popular saying "put yourself in my shoes?" I have worn those shoes, ladies. I understand your concerns and I'm here to help you overcome all those fears.

Always remember this -- don't give up on yourself! If you have a story to tell, be patient with yourself... with your life... with your ideas. It will happen and you will be able to share it with the world soon enough. Promise. You WILL win at writing!

There are sooo many parts to SUCCESSFULLY writing a book. I capitalized the word "successfully" because when you finish reading this book, that is what I want you to do. I want you to SUCCESSFULLY understand what you need in order to get your book completed. *Completed* meaning, you will be able to narrow down your idea and get an outline started. Or, *completed* meaning, you have a better understanding as to what is involved with writing a book and these explanations were just what you needed.

I believe that it is in you. I believe that you have this book in your hand and you are reading this very page because you are determined to WIN at writing! You want the tools and that little bit of "secret sauce" to get this writing thang done! And I'm going to see to it that you do just that.

Within these pages, we are going to break down some of the myths that make it *appear* that writing a book is impossible. We are going to show you how to WIN at writing and editing. It's nothing super complicated. Yes, you have to put in the work and be dedicated to the writing process, but if you stay the course? Your book WILL be written.

These are surefire tips, tools, and strategies that will work for beginners all the way to seasoned writers who might just want a brush-up on their writing and editing skills. (You're never too old to learn & enhance, right?) When you know better, you can do better, and when you do better you are set up to WIN!

Sometimes it's just having stuff spelled out and explained in a "few different" ways that make sense to *your* brain, which can be the "light bulb" moment for you. I get it. I understand. I'm the same way. Tell me in a way that is simple and ABC-123. Don't make it all scientific and theoretic... now you've lost me.

In this book we keep it simplified and designed so you can read it while sipping your coffee or tea in the morning or on your lunch break, or for those of us who know what it's like to steal away for a few minutes? Take it in the bathroom with you and read while soaking in the tub or even in your closet on the floor... wherever you can find some peace and no kid, family, boo thang or pet distractions! (I understand completely! LOL)

If there is something specific that may not be addressed, you can always reach out to me and the *Your Writing Table team* at: support@yourwritingtable.com. We will be glad to help in any we can.

Commonly Used Words

Throughout this book, there will be words and terms used that describe the book writing process. Some of you may be familiar with these words; those of you that are brand new to writing, welcome to the Wonderful World of Writing!

Manuscript: Your in-progress or completed book/story

Format & Layout: Process used to put your manuscript into correct position for printing (putting the book into the desired print size, positioning page numbers, line spacing, etc.)

Dims: Also known as "dimensions" or what the size of your book will be. Most of the time it will be 6x9 inches, however, you can discuss with your editor what size will work best for your book.

Header: The words at the top of each page; usually the author's name & book title or chapter titles

Footer: The words at the bottom of each page; usually page numbers are in this location. Reference information such as footnotes can also be placed in this position.

Font/Typeface: The text characters (letters and numbers) used to print your book

Spine: The part of the book that is visible when it stands in a closed position on a shelf/leaned against other books. It usually includes book title and author name.

Avatar: Mostly used in non-fiction books; a character you create to help you determine who your book is for (the ideal reader/client).

Part I:
Winning at Writing

The Idea

Your idea is amazing! It is the perfect book. It's gonna provide so much information and your business is going to explode once all your potential clients get a hold of it. Or it's gonna be the hottest, most sizzling romantic thriller that has ever hit the bookshelves and your followers are going to increase like never before.

Your idea is your "**why.**" What is the reason you are writing this book? What is your goal? This is especially important for those writing non-fiction. What message are you sending to the readers? Why do they need to read your book? What information are they going to receive while reading? Your "**why**" is your plot or central theme/reason for your book.

The only problem? How in the world do you get these fabulous ideas from your head to words that make sense and form them into an actual book? Here is step #1: **Just Write**.

That's it. I'll say it again in case you think I missed some words or it seemed too easy.

Step #1 – Just Write!

Without an idea, there is no book. The first part to creating the pages… creating the content… you gotta **<u>WRITE</u>**. It doesn't have to be in order, and it doesn't even have to make sense. Simply write down your thoughts while they are fresh in your mind. One of the hardest things is to write when your mind is blank, and/or you aren't able to recall any of the ideas that were once right at the forefront of your mind.

How to accomplish step #1: Set aside time when you can release your brain of all the ideas that have gathered. Some may call this a "brain dump" or "brain release."

NOTE: This method may seem wrong or "unorthodox" to some, however, there is no specific "right" or "wrong" way to write a book. YOU are the writer, so the creativity and *how* the creativity flows have to work for you. In addition, these are suggestions and tips that have worked for me and YWT clients. Most of all, embrace what inspires you!

The purpose of this writing activity is to allow you to literally be free to write in no specific order or pattern. It is to give you the opportunity to place all the puzzle pieces on the table, if you will. When you begin working on a jigsaw puzzle, you have to look at the loose, unorganized pieces then begin to put them in order - as it works for you - to form a complete puzzle. Whether it's a notebook and you are handwriting or it's on your smartphone or laptop… set aside some time and get into your "zone." Tap into that creative place in your mind and write down everything that is present. Again, it doesn't matter if it's not in order or if you have multiple paragraphs on different topics/subjects. These are the puzzle "pieces."

When I was working on the sequel for my very first fiction novel, I used this very process. I wrote the ideas as they came to me. I typed them on the computer, printed them out, and gave that set of ideas a title. I kept doing that and pretty soon I had all my chapters. I put them in order, added here and there, and made some more changes, then guess what? I had the book pretty much complete. Doing it this way took the pressure off me to have to write "in order" or to write a particular way. I wrote as I needed to for *me*, and it also allowed me to stay in my creative zone.

(NOTE: Fiction books are different from non-fiction books, so this type of brain release may not be as effective for a non-fiction book. We will discuss this in a later section.)

Writing is a **creative** process. You want to have fun with it, while also including some strategies to help you stay focused and disciplined as well. Releasing your ideas is a strategy that is in the beginning stages of creating your book, the content.

As a "creative," (if you identify yourself as this type of being), our brains don't work like our analytical or logical cousins. Creatives are a bit more free-spirited and tend to move on inspiration, imagination, and the multi-*shades* of gray versus just black & white. Being a "creative" you know that your brain flows freely, which lets you explore topics and themes that lead to characters, ideas, and pieces of literary work that bring joy to your heart. This type of creativity is needed when writing, especially if you're working on a fictional book. For those writing non-fiction, here is an activity you can do to help release your ideas. (For my fiction folks – stay tuned, the next section has what you need.)

Think of your ideas as a flower that branches out as your ideas begin to develop.

The middle square, "Your Idea," can be thought of as the seed... you don't have a flower (or book) without a seed, a starting point. Each of the squares extending from the starting point is a topic, idea, or question to ask while you're narrowing down your idea.

These are examples, of course. Feel free to add what works for you while you are creating. Remember, these are *your* thoughts and you're writing this book in *your* way, in *your* words!

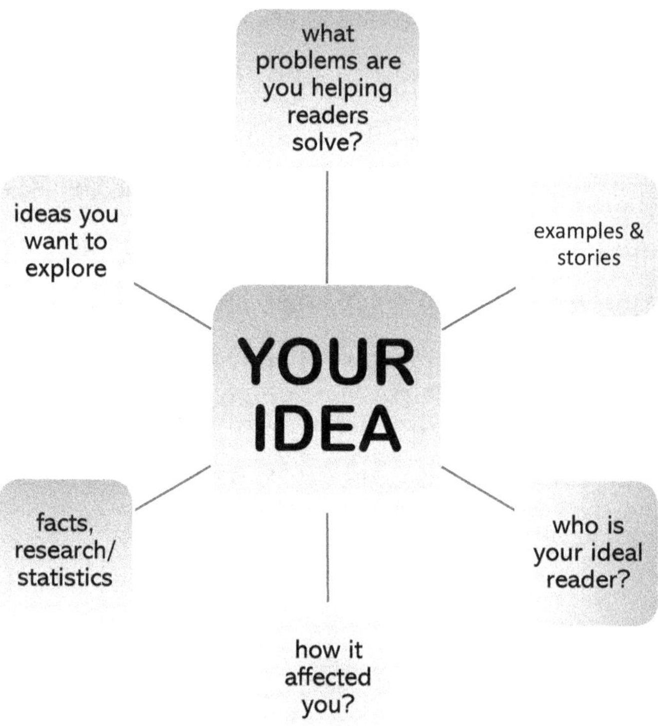

Non-Fiction Idea Flower: use this to help sort your ideas and "map" out the direction you want your book to go.

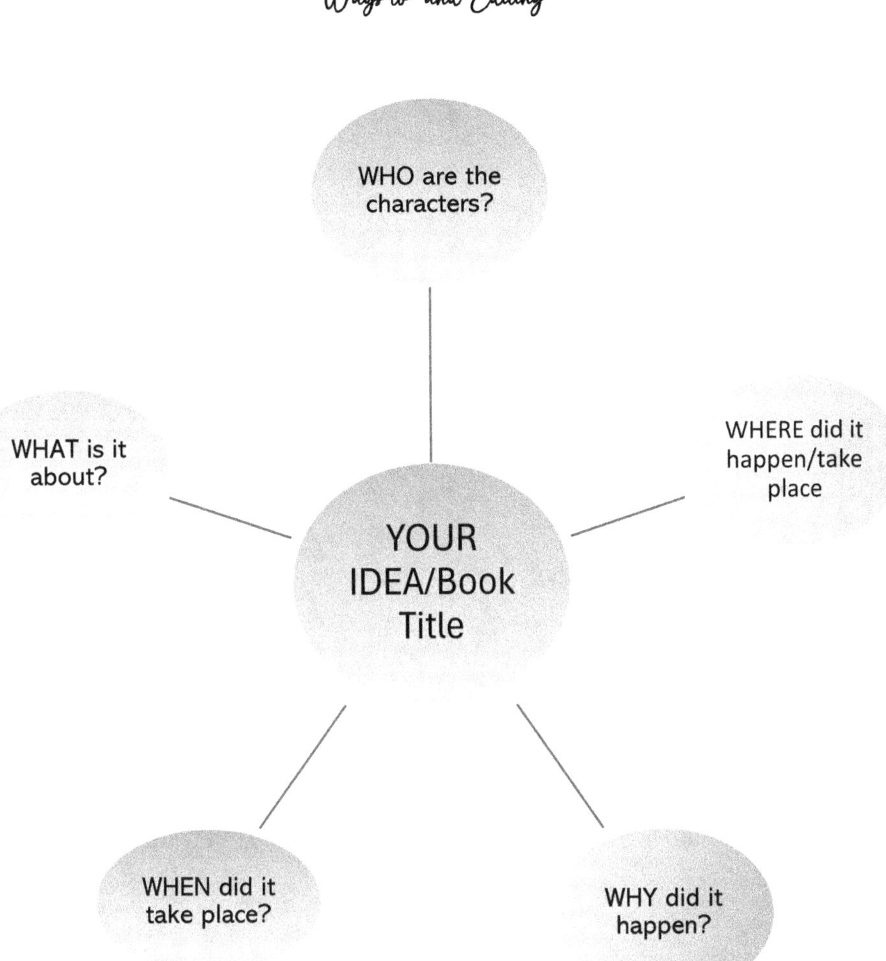

Fiction Idea Flower: use this to help sort your fiction story ideas based on characters, plot & setting

Writing the Vision: Using vision boards

When you think of vision boards, the first thought is usually a board where you are finding pictures and words/phrases that will inspire, motivate and get you hyped about achieving goals and dreams that you have set for your life or career. You can use this same concept for writing. This also works for all genres and non-fiction. (We will cover fiction and non-fiction separately, don't worry.)

When creating a writer's vision board, you want to include pictures/images, words, phrases that connect with your book idea. For example, if you are writing a fictional book and it's a romantic thriller/suspense about a woman who falls in love with a guy she met in the grocery store parking lot. They develop a relationship, and he finds out she's a stalker who leaves fresh fruit and produce at his front door three times a day. The title is "Keep Your Fruit." (that title is poppin', right? LOL If you use it for your own book, can you shout me out in your Acknowledgement section, k? LOL no, seriously… let me know so I can cheer you on!)

Build your vision board like this: Have a designated space for each thing you want to focus on: characters, setting, plot, climax, etc.

Character Development

Your largest section/focus will most likely be on your characters or "character development" when writing a fictional book. It is so, so critical that you take time to think about the characters and how you want to develop/create them so readers will be able to relate to them and identify. For example, our lady meets the guy in the grocery store parking lot, right? We need to have a whole personality and identity created for these characters because not only are they the MAIN characters, but you want to have an idea already composed in *your* mind about who they are.

So, this lady is in her mid-30s, her name is Maisie, has been through a lot of bad relationships that left her bitter and broken. She wants to trust, but she doesn't know how to and now she wants to be in control of everything. She has taken on a very dangerous and somewhat aggressive attitude when it comes to dating.

You also want to include how the characters look: height, weight, hair color, skin tone, eye color, any tattoos, body piercings, etc. All of these specific details are "building" the character and will help you also stay focused when writing certain scenes that require details. The details are what will make the difference in the success of your book because readers will love the fact that you took the time to present characters that are not general and vague. You want your book to be so detailed that readers can literally "see" and imagine the characters you are describing through words like they are watching a movie. Details will allow your characters to POP off the pages and come to life as the reader is going page by page.

Here is a table you can set up on your vision board as an example to create individual characters:

Character Name:
Nickname (if applicable):

Physical description (what do they look like: height, weight, hair style/type, etc):

Their strengths/what hypes them up:

Their weaknesses/what pushes their buttons:

What's their background (upbringing, family/people who were around them, where they were born, etc)

You can also create how the main characters met. This will help you to remember what brought them together; their positive energy and also what may be negative or toxic about their interaction. Those small, but critical details can add so many wonderful layers to each character which brings your story to life. Small things like they both may be addicted to drugs or something like that can add complexity and help the reader to understand why they are drawn to each other, but they are toxic and no good for each other at the same time.

Characters:
How they met (include where/time of year, etc. Be as specific as possible so readers are literally in the scene with you):

Any past relationship baggage/trauma?
Any toxic behaviors?
Do either of them have kids?
What is their credit like?
Do they have a car?
What is their living situation? Rent/own? Alone or roomies?
Do they have commitment issues?
Do they smoke/drink?
Who are their closest friends/inner circle?

When I wrote my first novel, *"Antithesis"* (no longer available for purchase), I developed one of the main characters, Tarell, so well that I actually despised him! LOL I hated everything about him. And the readers felt the same way because they told me in their feedback that they couldn't stand him. I was so thrilled because that meant I understood the assignment! You want your readers to identify, relate to and truly believe that these characters have "real" personalities. **#itsAllintheDetail**
Before we go to the next section of the vision board, in addition to writing the words to describe the

characters, you can also look for images, pictures that represent your character. For example, if Maisie has an olive-toned complexion and her hair is kinky/curly to compliment her dark brown eyes and chiseled cheekbones, you can search the internet for pictures of women that look close to this description. Having this image on the board will also keep Maisie's character fresh in your mind while writing about her. You can also do "brain release" activities on your characters. You can write a few pages on their background which you can incorporate into the story if you wish. All of these things add depth and more personality for the readers to identify with.

Story Background/Setting

This is very important, too, because this will give you the setting of where the story takes place. You want to include the year - is it present day or years ago? Setting the time period will also help you stay focused on how you describe locations, clothing that characters are wearing, types of cars being driven or mentioned, etc. The setting also lets the reader know what to look for in the story and they will be able to understand how/why certain things are described in a particular way.

You also want to include the location - city, state, country, etc. For example, Maisie met the guy in the grocery store parking lot. She was wearing leggings and a sweatshirt as it was the middle of November, and the weather was cool. She had just left the gym and it was about 9am, so it was slightly windy as was the temperature for this time of year in Chicago/Midwest region.

If you are not sure of a location's weather/atmosphere, it is recommended that you research that city/state/country to be sure you are as accurate as possible when writing your story. You want all of your details to be correct, which will allow the story to be rich and engrossing for your reader.

Plot

This is definitely critical This is definitely critical just like character development. The plot is the storyline... what the book is going to be about. It is the sequence of events that keeps the readers engaged and excited about your book. There is a beginning, middle, and end like that in a movie.

For our example story, Maisie meets the guy in the parking lot, then she secretly follows him to his home. Meeting in the parking lot is the first event, then following him home is the next event. Another plot example is a rags to riches story… the main character starts out poor/financially challenged and by the end of the book, they go to Vegas and win a major jackpot on one of the slot machines. As you continue to develop the ideas, you will provide more keywords, images, and anything else that will help you to prepare your story.

In the box below, you will see how you can add this to your vision board as well to help you stay focused on the plot/story idea. It's really easy to get lost once you start writing and you can forget your original idea. Placing this on your vision board/story notes is a great way to keep it in front of you!

You can also refer to your other board/story notes if you need help remembering character descriptions and your thoughts for how you want the characters to flow throughout the story.

The summary of the story is:

Main characters & their description/backgounds
(List those things you wrote in the character development section – strengths, weaknesses of each & what do they both have in common with each other)

What are the goals they are both striving for?
Are they achievable or just pipe dreams?

Have they made any efforts to achieve their goals?
If yes, what were those efforts?
If no, what were the failures/missed opportunities?

Use these spaces to begin creating your own vision board… have fun exploring and bringing your ideas to life!

Character Name:

Nickname (if applicable):

Physical description (what do they look like: height, weight, hair style/type, etc.):

Their strengths/what hypes them up:

Their weaknesses/what pushes their buttons:

What's their background (upbringing, family/people who were around them, where they were born, etc.)

Background/story setting:

Time of year (month/year)

Character connection/relationship with each other:

Non-fiction Planning

For all my non-fiction writers, you don't write a "plot" per se. Yes, you still have to narrow down your ideas and your themes, but your set up will be a bit different. Non-fiction books have a wide range of topics from self-help, how-to's/DIYs to memoirs and biographies to politics, religion, and social/cultural awareness.

There is always something to write about when it comes to non-fiction and the content primarily comes from research and observation. There is still a beginning, middle and end for your book and they are referred to as the opening (or set-up, the WHY), conflict (bringing in the problem, the WHAT) and the solution (how to solve the problem, the HOW.)

Opening/WHY (Beginning)

The awesome thing about non-fiction books is they do not have to start chronologically or in a specific order. You can decide what the beginning of the book/story will be. Just like a fictional book, you want to draw readers and pique their interest as soon as they start reading the first page.

In your opening, you will introduce the subject/ main topic. You can talk about its significance to you and how it has affected you. This will be your set up for the content in the book. The opening is also how you identify and state the purpose of the book and what readers will learn from the book. Is the purpose to inform, entertain or persuade readers to do something? Keeping this in mind will also help you to stay focused while writing.

Conflict/WHAT (Middle)

Here is where you will present the problem that you are solving for the reader. Describe what the problem/issue/ conflict is that you are addressing. You can go into greater detail of the issue at hand, which will allow the reader to see that you understand their issue.

Solution/HOW (Ending)

Provide the steps and/or explanations as to how the issue will be solved. Provide results, examples of others who have tried your method and were successful. It is always a plus to include your own experiences as well.

This makes it personal and lets the reader know you identify with them.

Before you actually begin writing, take some time to narrow down your ideas and confirm what you will finally write about. You can also make a list of sub-topics that you want to discuss, and this will allow you to be sure that you don't skip anything you want to discuss. Sub-topics will also allow you to think about questions you want to answer and problems you want to solve for the reader. Write down ALL ideas in these beginning stages. NO IDEA IS A BAD OR DUMB IDEA! Remember that. 😊

Creating an outline before you begin writing is also a good idea. It's not necessary and some people don't require an outline, but it is an effective tool for organization and time management. For example, I used an outline while writing this very book and others. I did not have a Table of Contents at the beginning, but by the time I was almost done creating the content, the chapter titles came easy. Here is a sample outline to give you an idea on how to break down what you will write about:

I. Introduction

II. How to start your own auto detailing business
       a. research the area where you want to work
       b. think about target audience
       c. pros & cons to having a location vs providing mobile services
III. Forming the business – what's needed
       a. supplies needed
       b. business account
       c. sole proprietor or LLC?
       d. work alone or have a business partner
IV. Advertising & promoting the business
       a. work with branding mgr
       b. using social media
V. Conclusion

There is no right or wrong outline… there is no right or wrong order to list the things you will discuss. You may decide to add more sections or you may feel that part III, section b should be switched and put in another part of the book. It's okay! This outline is to help you stay focused once you have narrowed down your idea – that's it. Feel free to change anything you choose. **#itsYOURbook**

Writing Strategies

This is critical to not just writing a book, but in all writing projects. Yes, as we stated earlier, writing is a creative process. As a writer, YOU are a ***creative***. Yes, you want to be sure you are "inspired" and in your "zone" when you start writing, but you also want to be sure you are maximizing your writing time and being as efficient as possible while writing. Some find it easier to create an outline to use for writing, and others are more spontaneous with no outline. Whichever works for you, be consistent and be focused! That will be the key to completing your book in a timely manner. Let's look at a few strategies you may find helpful.

Create an avatar

This is a method that works really well for non-fiction books rather than fiction books. This is because fiction books already have a plot, story idea and concept. Character development and all the other factors will add to the story to make it complete. Non-fiction, on the other hand, can be a bit more challenging as you will need to be sure "who" your target audience is. When creating the content, you have to keep in mind "who" you are writing the book for.

Creating an **avatar**, or a fancy word for saying "character," will help you to determine who your book is for – who is the perfect person to buy and read your book. By doing this it will help you to understand exactly who your ideal reader is so you can write a book/create a message that will provide the solution that makes sense to your perfect reader/customer. The avatar is a perfect representation of the ideal customer that will buy your book.

I have an avatar for each book that I write. I know exactly who I'm writing to and writing for. When I get stuck, I think of the avatar (or put the image on my screen so it's right in front of me) and I literally imagine they are sitting next to me or we're on the phone and I'm sharing the info with them. Avatars truly help me stay focused and remember my "why." And make the avatar look however you want! They are your inspiration and client focus-point while writing. This is something we have our clients do as well so they can visualize their ideal reader and stay focused on their main idea. You can find images on Google by using search words "free stock images ___". (Add the description of the type of person you are looking for based on the idea/message of your book. Example: working woman, depressed woman, career woman, etc.)

While you are creating your avatar, keep these things in mind:

WHO is going to be the best person/group of people to buy your book? Those people are your "target" audience. We need to create the "avatar" to help keep the vision in your mind of "who" you are writing your book for.

Creating your avatar means you should know everything about them... as if they were your best friend. By doing this, you will be an expert on how to write your book, what to say and how to say it, which will speak directly to your reader and motivate them to buy your book!

Here is an example of an avatar. Remember, you can search the internet to find sample photos of the men/women who best represent your client. It doesn't have to be perfect, k? ☺

Based on what your book is about, you can look at this lady and see that she may fit a topic discussing women's issues such as parenting or relation-trips. She appears to be frustrated or sad or stressed out. She could be a single mom due to divorce or never married & dealing with "baby daddy" drama. She could be married and having problems in her marriage… maybe she lost her job and is struggling to find a new job to take care of her kids and pay bills.

You are in control of creating her entire situation and description!

Her name is Chanelle. She is in her late 30's and works at a doctor's office as an office manager. She is married with 2 kids ages 10 and 7, boy and girl. Her marriage is pretty good… she and her husband have been married for 5 years but known each other since high school. They have their issues like all couples, but he supports her,

and she loves him. They try to do things as a family when they can. A lot of times the kids are home during summer and school breaks playing outside or fighting over the TV like most siblings do.

Her goal is to start her own beauty supply store to provide products for her local community. The closest quality beauty supply is at least 20 minutes away and their products are trash and there is not a wide variety of things to choose from. She is already working with vendors to learn about how to purchase supplies. She is also working with a realtor to get information on purchasing a store space and the best location to do so.

Chanelle is a hard worker and doesn't wait for other people to help her out. When she gets an idea, she rolls with it to get it done. She believes that knowledge is power so once she gets her supply store started, she wants to provide training for young girls on becoming an entrepreneur, and classes on hair and makeup. She is looking to work with other business owners to partner and give back to the community.

Get the idea? You make the avatar/ideal reader who you NEED and WANT them to be. Whatever you need your "avatar" to be, you are able to create it. The goal is to create a character that will help you to stay on track while writing your book and helping you to remember your "why."

This example avatar provides the visual image of the client you're thinking about and then the description or personality of that client is provided. Your description is going to help you remember your WHY and WHAT you are writing about. If you could share your information with the perfect person, what would you say? What do they look like? That's what you want to keep in mind.

Plan/outline vs pantsing

As we have discussed previously, there are different ways to get your content written for your book. Some like outlines and some don't. Creating an outline is one of the most common ways to help you plan what you're going to write. You can list the possible chapter titles, subjects and everything you want to discuss in that section, then write each section until they are all complete. Outlines are a very effective way to get your book written. Not only does it help you to not miss anything, but you can schedule your writing time based on how many chapters will be in the book. 8 chapters? You can do one chapter per day, and you can have the content completed in 8 days. If you get inspired, you may complete it sooner than that.

Here is an outlining tool that you can use which may work great for you: It's called "Plottr" and it walks you step-by-step in creating your outline: (Link/web address is at the back of the book.)

If outlines do not work for you, you probably prefer to write as ideas come to your mind. This is like a freestyle and there is a literary slang term which describes this, and it's known as "pantsing." This basically means writing without an outline. Writers who are creating fictional novels are more likely to write in this pattern versus non-fiction books, but pantsing is not limited to any specific genre.

Remember that it is a fancy name for writing with no outline. If you write better with no outline, go for it! Writing is creative and it's all about how YOU are inspired and what gets you going. Outlines do provide discipline and structure, but again, if ain't your thing, no worries. Keep writing and tell your story YOUR way in YOUR words in YOUR style! (I've written a couple books with no outline… it worked for me at that time! LOL)

I'm sure some of you have heard of "NaNoWriMo?" It is a non-profit organization based in northern California that supports creative writing, and they have programs that support fluency and education. They are most known for their annual 30-day writing challenge, which is where their name came from: National Novel Writing Month. Every year on November 1 (since 1999) they challenge writers to begin creating a novel and writing at least 50,000 by November 30. Thousands of people join this challenge every year and some are very successful. (For more information, check out their website: https://nanowrimo.org/)

Since so many people join this challenge every year, there are those who are familiar with writing and they may create an outline to follow, and of course there are first-time writers who have no idea of a formal writing structure, so they just start with whatever is on their mind. NaNoWriMo understands writers come from all walks of life and some use outlines and some don't, and they did provide a general outline that anyone can use to begin writing their book. See below. (You can get more info by visiting the NaNoWriMo website.)

Step 1: Write down your idea
Step 2: Write a summary of that idea
Step 3: Divide your idea into parts
Step 4: Map each of those ideas into smaller parts

Recording your book vs writing/typing

Creating the content for your book can be done in a number of ways. Before the wonderful invention of computers and word processing software such as Microsoft Word, you had to handwrite or use an actual typewriter. Now, you can use your desktop, laptop, smartphone, or tablet/iPad to get your content written.

There are recording features such as talk-to-text which allow you to speak, talk and the computer/app will take the audio and convert it into the written text/words via auto transcription. Transcription, for those who aren't familiar with the term, is taking audio and turning it into written words. (*Your Writing Table* does provide this service as well!)

Google Docs has a feature: CTRL+SHIFT+S which turns on the voice typing feature. There are also apps such as: Speechnotes, Evernote, Otter Voice Notes and more. These three are some of the more popular ones and they can be downloaded on your phone or table.

- ✓ **Speechnotes** – this app is FREE, and you can email and text your document to yourself or whomever you choose. You can create new "notes" in the app and every "note" is also backed up and sent to Google Drive. (You connect it to your Gmail email address.)
- ✓ **Evernotes** - this app has different plans to fit your needs: free and paid. There are multiple features such as calendar, creating templates, syncing and organizing, and even a document

scanner. (All features may not be available based on the plan you select.) This app works on desktop/laptop and smartphones.

✓ **Otter Voice Notes** also has different plans to fit your needs. There is a free version and there are paid plans as well. This app works on your computer as well as iPhones & Androids. Just as Google Docs & Speechnotes, Otter will allow you to speak your content and it will convert/transcribe it into written text.

As with all transcription apps, please be sure to go back and review what was transcribed. Your words may not be recorded correctly and that could mess up your document. For example, you may have spoken: "the cat walked over the fence and hissed at the dog." The transcription may record: "the cat walked hovering the mints and spit chat dog" or something that was not correct. The reason this happens could be for various reasons: you may have been speaking too low and the microphone did not pick up your words; you may have been speaking too fast; there may have been background noise; you may have an accent when you talk, and the microphone did not understand a word that you said. It is important to speak slowly and make sure your mouth is close to the microphone. Also be sure you are in a quiet area to reduce the risk of background noise being picked up.

Be sure to check the transcription frequently while recording. You may want to check what is being transcribed every 2-3 sentences so you can make the corrections while that thought is still fresh in your mind. I have experienced this many times when I was recording, and it didn't transcribe the right way. I recorded for about 3-4 minutes and when I looked back at the words, there were so many errors. Unfortunately, I didn't remember some of the thoughts and I was talking too fast because I was trying to get the idea out before I forgot. The sentences were totally wrong and some of the words were so off that I couldn't remember what I was trying to say originally.

Overall, these recording apps are AMAZING and they are great time-savers. If you don't have time to sit at your desk or sit down, period… you can record your content while you're riding in the car or sitting outside on your patio. Before you know it, you have your book written – on your phone! And you all have to do is email it to yourself. That's awesome, right?

One more thing! If you do prefer handwriting, please convert the handwritten content into a digital format such as Word or Google Docs. When it's time for editing to begin, the editor/publisher cannot use your handwritten notes.

Again, if you don't want to type, you can use one of the audio recording apps and just read your notes out loud. You can send that converted version to the editor. Everything must be in digital format as that is what will be uploaded for the printer.

Notes...

Titles & Covers...

The phrase is cliché and you've heard it a gazillion times, even outside of conversations about books: Don't judge a book by its cover. However, as a writer (or aspiring writer), you should *definitely* judge your cover. The cover of your book and the title of your book should not be overlooked. They can be seen or thought of as a partnership. Titles and book covers work jointly with "selling" and "attracting" your reader. I know, I know... many of you don't even start writing the content until you have the title, right? And that's great! You definitely want to be sure the title of your book is just what you want it to be so it can serve a few purposes. We'll talk about them in just a minute.

Book covers are also SUPER DUPER important! The cover is probably more important than the title for many reasons as well. If that is something you have been struggling with or have lots of questions, this section is for you!

Tackling the TITLE!

- ✓ What in the world should you call your book?
- ✓ Should you use big, complicated words?
- ✓ Should you keep it simple?
- ✓ Should you add a subtitle? What is a subtitle?
- ✓ Should the font be capital letters or in cursive/script?
- ✓ Does it matter what color the letters/words are?

These are just a few of the questions that arise when it's time to start thinking of your book title. Whether it's fiction or non-fiction, memoir or self-help, your book's title should be catchy while also letting the reader know what the book will be about. The reason you should have a good (or great) title is to pull potential readers in and generate interest without giving away too much of what the book is about.

When you present your book to the world, you say a little bit of the book is about and you say the title. The title should be the "hook" that gets the audience's attention right away. The title is also one of your most critical marketing tools because it's your conversation piece while discussing and promoting it. Sometimes readers will buy your book after they hear the title or read it on the book cover.

Take some time to really think about the title of your book. The words can evoke emotion, attitude, or mystery, and it's what potential readers take with them about the book from the beginning. Your title is part of your book's first impression and you want it to be a good one!

The question is often asked on "how" the title should be created… should it be a couple words, one word that has a lot of impact, maybe a quote from one of the chapters?? The answer is basically make it unique, easy to understand, authentic to YOU and your voice but it should grab the reader's attention. It should be a show-stopper, pretty much! LOL

Here is an example of what NOT to do! When I wrote my first fiction novel in 2005, I was working with an independent publisher who was just getting started in the literary world. She was super pumped to help me get my first book out and I was also going to be her first publishing project for her brand. We were stuck on the title and we played around with many possibilities. I don't know why but I agreed with her suggestion of a one-word title. No problem with the one-word thing… it would create impact. Got it. But the word that was chosen??? The title was "*Antithesis*" and the subtitle was "Finding Balance in the Midst of Opposition." Say whattttt??

First of all, the one-word "antithesis" was hard for *me* to say! If I, the author, couldn't pronounce the word what would potential readers think? I did question my publisher and I asked was she sure that this was the title we needed to use, and she was all for it! Even the subtitle sounded like a college paper or some type of report.

Needless to say, I didn't promote it like I should have and I know that was because I was not comfortable with the title. You have to be comfortable and secure with the title you select. It should roll off your tongue smoothly when you say it and repeat it. It should give you a positive surge of energy and excitement when you think about it and talk about it with others. You can also look at other titles in the genre you're writing in to get ideas. See what other authors have done and get inspired from their work.

For example, if you're writing about poetry, look at some of your favorite poets and see what titles they came up with. If you're writing urban fiction, look at your favorite authors or authors in that genre and see what they have used for titles. Don't make it super hard on yourself to come up with something if you're stuck. How does that phrase go? Don't reinvent the wheel? So, give your brain a break and look at what others have done, get some ideas and go from there. You got this!

When it comes to subtitles, it is *optional*, but it can give LIFE to your title and kick your book cover up a few notches. Subtitles are more commonly used for non-fiction books to give more explanation to what the book is about. It is usually 3-7 words long, but for non-fiction it may be longer, like 10 words. A great subtitle is where you can create your "hook," so to speak and really let the reader know – in a few words – what the book is about without having read to read the blurb/description on the back cover or the inside.

You want it to be specific and bold, again, to catch the attention of the interested reader. One way to think of a subtitle is like your "salesperson" for your book. That one line of a few words can draw or repel a reader.

For fiction books, subtitles can be as simple or as short as "A Novel," or "A Memoir," or "A Gut-busting Romantic Comedy." For non-fiction books, you want to be more specific. One of my books is titled, *"Say It Right: 5 Tools for Effective Communication."* It is short, bold, clear and the reader knows what the book is about and what they will learn while reading the book.

Creating that killer COVER!
An amazing book cover is the other half to your book presentation and deal-closer for readers. The title and book cover go hand-in-hand; they are a partnership. One "can" work without the other, but majority of the time, they work **together**. I know there are times when I decide if I want to read a book simply based on the image of the cover OR the title. Other times, I have to look at both, read the description on the back cover, then decide. Think of it like this: if someone has to take time to read the description *and* look at the cover *and* re-read the title, they may lose interest.

The goal of a dynamic book cover is to "sell" the reader immediately. You want to communicate your idea to the reader. The book cover IS your signature statement! It IS what can make or break a reader; especially if they are new to your work. Book cover design is absolutely critical to what will get your book more sales or few sales. It's the truth. This is why I said at the beginning of this section, it is a totally cliché statement, but yes – books ARE judged by their covers. You **want** to judge your book cover, and you are authorized to do so. It is highly recommended and suggested.

Just like the title, your book cover is literally your first impression with potential readers. It is one of the most important aspects of marketing and advertising your book. If a reader is short on time or they are just moving quickly to pick up a good read, the cover is one of the things that will stand out and help them make that decision.

For example, how many times have you been at the airport and you forgot your book/magazine at home? You go to the newsstand inside the terminal and they have books and magazines on display. There may be authors you know, but there are usually a handful of authors you don't know. So, you have to rely on the images/pictures/font and word style on the cover to help you decide.

For books written by celebrities, public figures such as athletes or political leaders, you may be drawn to their book just because of their photo on the cover. Outside of those types of covers, the artwork, color scheme, word/font style are all significant when it comes to book cover design. If you are writing a horror book, your cover should have something to do with the content. It should be dark, gory, and maybe include scary images which will let your reader know immediately what the book is about. If you are writing contemporary rom-com (romantic comedy), your cover may have light, pastel colors, script/cursive words and illustrated characters to reflect the light, humorous content.

Again, as we discussed in the previous section on titles… if you are stuck and can't come up with anything, don't stress yourself. Look at other authors in the same genre, see what they have done and get inspiration and ideas from them. **#DON'Treinventthewheel**

Here are some things for you to think about while designing our book cover:

- ✓ Does it represent your story or message?
- ✓ Does it promote intrigue or interest?
- ✓ Does it stand out/look different from other books in the same genre?
- ✓ Are you using textures and patterns for additional details that are not distracting?
- ✓ Do you have **successful** composition? (Are all your images, font, graphics and colors coming together effectively?)

There is software available (ranging from free to expensive) that will help you design a book cover, however, if you are not comfortable with graphic design or illustrations, it is suggested that you hire a graphics designer or someone skilled in designing book covers. The reason for this is because someone who has expertise in the area of graphic design will know how to use the right colors, size for the images, the right type of font/typeface that will be the most impactful and effective for the cover.

In addition, remember this: book covers work TOGETHER with the title. They literally compliment and play off each other. The title should be one that grabs the reader's attention and compels them to purchase it because it was bold, visible, clear and straight to the point. The cover added to their interest because of its pops of vibrant color, the bold block capital letters in bright red on a gold background along with an image of an explosion and other visual elements strengthened the cover perfectly.

Lastly, you don't want to have too many visual images or the font you selected for your title and subtitle are not clear. You want to be able to combine everything to work together and keep your story/book idea in mind at all times. If you are working with a professional graphics designer, be sure that you are sharing your vision with them so they can create the cover that you see in your mind. You want that idea to come to life and manifest on the cover of your book!

Coach or no coach?

Only you will know if you need a coach/consultant to help you with writing your book. One can recommend a coach to you as well, but you are the only one to make the final decision. The purpose of hiring a coach/consultant is to receive structured guidance and assistance while writing your book. Their role is to also help you stay focused, challenge, stretch you and steer you in the right direction while writing your book.

What is the difference between a "coach" and a "consultant?" For the most part, they are pretty much the same. The writing coach & writing consultant both provide guidance, insight structured activities/ assignments designed to assist you with your writing idea to help you reach the ultimate goal of completing your book. A consultant brings more technical and focused strategies to solve the writing problems/issues compared to a coach that gives the author the tools to solve the writing problem themselves or come to their "own" solution on writing.

YWT provides consulting services, which means we are going to cover the technical and structured portions of your project, while also providing coaching strategies that will encourage and promote you to stretch your creative brain when it comes to your writing project.

When I am working with clients, we talk about their book project as a whole from their idea/vision on the content to the book cover design and what their goals are once the book is complete. I want to be sure they understand the entire process, especially when it comes to editing. Many writers/authors are extremely nervous when it comes to the editing phase and I walk with them step by step to be sure they understand, and are comfortable, with how everything will go.

You may also feel you need a coach/ consultant if you are stuck and cannot get past an idea or concept. Maybe you have the idea in your mind, but you really don't know "how" to put those ideas into written form. Your coach/consultant will be able to guide you and give you specific activities or "homework" to help you cross your writing hurdles.

The assignments "…make everything seem so simple… the exercises and tools help you to get started on your book and push you to pull yourself out of your creative block. I didn't realize how working with a consultant would help me accomplish my goal of writing a book." That was what Maham Choudry, YWT editing client and soon-to-be published author, had to say about her experience of hiring us to assist her with her book-writing project.

There *is* a financial investment when hiring a coach/consultant. They can range from hundreds of dollars to thousands. You are paying for not only their time, but their expertise and knowledge in the area of book writing. You are paying them to assist you with completing your book. Again, do your research! Get information on the coaches/consultants you are interested in and talk with them. Look at their websites and see what services they provide, their rates and their testimonials. What their clients have to say is just as important as how much they charge. If their clients have left positive reviews, that is something you can make note of. You can also ask for references to see what other colleagues, previous clients or partners have to say about them.

There may be packages or courses offered by the coach/consultant that will be perfect for your writing project. You may need to meet with them once or twice to get you started or get you "unstuck" on an idea. You may need to watch their course online which may answer all your questions. Talking with them, visiting their website and even seeing if they have a social media presence can make the difference in making your decision to work with them.

Before signing a contract or agreement, set up a consultation and have a conversation so you can see if your personalities work together. If anything is not comfortable and trustworthy to you, move on to the next coach/consultant. Also, if you know people who have worked with them before, speak with them. They can give you the "real deal" compared to what may be shown on a website or social media.

Correcting the Myths

When you start writing your book, it's normal – and OKAY – to have questions. You hear stories from other writers or you read something, or you see something on social media. Ladies always have something they want cleared up when it comes to their writing and most of the time, it's one of those "is this true?" kindsa questions. So, I wanted to break down a couple of them for you… these are some of the most common questions asked.

Myth or Truth? I should have a degree or some type of professional training/education in order to write a book - **MYTH**

You do not have to have a college degree or any type of professional or accredited certification in order to write a book. There are courses you can take to help you get started writing your book, but definitely not necessary.

If you are going to write something that will include facts, statistics or educational/learning type of content, you need to be sure you are knowledgeable of the subject, which can be from your own experience or you are using information from other sources. If you are writing a fictional book, you are creating the characters, setting and everything that goes on with the storyline. You are in full control from start to finish. No degree needed. Imagination and ideas are your only requirement.

Myth or Truth? It takes one year or longer to write a complete book. – **BOTH** ☺

Depending on your level of commitment can determine how long it will take you to complete writing your book. I have written a full book in 3 years and I have written a book in 3 days. The one that took years was because I stopped and started, life happened, and also the content was based on real life events so I literally had to "live" out the book before it could be written. The one that took days was a divine in which I literally sat and wrote until I was done. I didn't even realize it was a complete book. HAAA!!!

Some of the YWT clients have done the same thing: one wrote their book in about a week and another client wrote theirs in a couple months. One focused on writing every day and they had the time to do it. The other had to balance between working full time and the stop & start syndrome.

Also, some of you may have deadlines or time frames that you want to meet for events/book signings or speaking engagements and you want to have the book completed by then. It is all up to you. Deadlines can provide a sense of accountability and that may be what you need to finish. In other situations, you may need to write as it comes to you, and that's okay, too. Do what is comfortable for you while allowing you to work at the pace that's good for you.

Myth or Truth? I can actually write my book on my cell phone or other device – **TRUTH**

Technology has advanced so much that yes, you can write your book on your cell phone!! It's really a cool thing to do!

There are different apps that you can download on your phone which will allow you to speak and it will turn your words into text ("speech to text" is what it's called), and some will also allow you to type if you choose to as well.

When you are done recording, you will have the option to email yourself or another source or you can access your content. This type of technology has literally changed the game for so many writers because everyone is not able to sit at a desk or have access to a laptop. Others prefer to talk compared to typing. It's all about preference and if they make it easier to get your book done, that's what matters!

Myth or Truth? You have to have the title of your book and book cover design figured out before you start writing the book. – **MYTH**

You do not have to have the title or the book cover design when you start writing your book. Many of the YWT clients do not have these items when they start working with us. We discuss their ideas and some clients don't finalize their title or book cover until they are almost done creating the content.

Sometimes you need to complete the content in order to be comfortable with a title that pops, catches the attention of the reader and works with the content.

The book cover is the same concept – the idea may not come until the end of the content creation. We encourage clients to begin narrowing down their book cover design while we are at the beginning of the project so the design team can begin creating sketch drafts for the client to review. Depending on what the client wants (type of font, color scheme, illustrations or images, etc.) will determine how quickly the design team works. In addition, if the client wants a hand drawn illustration/image/cover art, that may take additional time as illustrations and other artwork are manually created compared to images that are computer originated.

Myth or Truth? I need to have all my ideas together before I start writing my book – **MYTH**

It's perfectly okay to not have all your ideas when you start writing. There are tools and strategies (such as the Idea Flower we talked about in the first chapter) that can help you to sort out everything and narrow down what you want to write about. Vision boards are also great tools to assist in sorting out what you want to write about.

Myth or Truth? I have to have really good writing skills/ know how to spell in order to write a book. -
MYTH

This is one of the biggest myths out there. No, you don't have to be a perfect speller or be a master at the English language to write a book. This is especially true if you are writing poetry or a fictional novel in which the characters and/or content have a particular style or type of language that may require "incorrect" spelling according to the dictionary or your English teacher's standards.

If you are writing about a hip hop rapper, for example, the way they would speak is most likely not going to be standard grammar. There will be lots of abbreviations, slang terms and things like that. Another example would be if you are writing a book that has a small child or someone from a foreign country. The language for these characters will not be standard, either.

The goal when you're creating characters is to release their identity and allow the reader to get to know them and connect with them. When you are giving them dialogue for their conversations with others, it is okay for you to have them say things that may not be grammatically correct. A technical writing term for that is called "colloquialism" and it means an informal language style that is used for everyday conversation/ communication between people.

When writing poetry, you may experience the same thing… the topic you may be writing about may not include standard English words. And that's okay. Stay true to your writing voice and how you want the reader to connect to your words.

When you are done creating your content, I recommend hiring an editor to look over everything and they can make the spelling, proofreading or other grammatical things that are noticed. They will be sure that the things you aren't sure about are corrected and perfected.

Part II:
Winning at EDITING

An Editor is your literary BFF

Editing gets a lot of mixed reviews. For some, they don't write anything without professional editing being done. For others, it's a bad word, they aren't needed, and a waste of money and resources. Whatever your personal opinion, hiring a professional editor is a highly recommended resource that assists writers in many capacities. I believe the reason why some feel editors are not needed is because they have had a negative experience, or they have not done their due diligence and taken the time to research what an editor actually is/does and how they can be beneficial to a writing project.

An editor's job is to "fine tune" the writer's manuscript or document. An editor looks at the work that is presented and they correct minor things such as missing periods, commas or apostrophes. They also look at more complex things such as developmental errors or relevancy – does this paragraph fit with the story line/plot/idea and things like that.

What is an editor is NOT supposed to do? This is where I believe writers have had negative experiences. An editor is NOT supposed to change the writer's voice or writing style. It is very important that an editor provide suggestions/ feedback on something they think should be changed rather than delete completely. If the editor sees something that they feel needs attention, they can make a suggestion and allow the writer to accept or reject the suggestion. At the end of the day, the editor has to remember it is up to the writer to make the final decision as to how they want their document to flow.

That brings us to our next point while talking about editors. This is something I discuss all the time with potential clients, colleagues and others, and that is this point: Editors should embrace the writer's vision from the beginning of the project. When researching and interviewing editors, they should "gel" or connect with the writer. There has to be a connection, so they are able to communicate freely among each other.

An editor is like that of a hair stylist, nail technician, barber, or even your dentist. They are coming into your personal space... your thoughts, visions, ideas, and depending on the genre/content, they are even talking with your family and friends who may be assisting with the project. It is critical that the editor and the writer develop a repor so the writer is comfortable sharing their ideas with the editor, and they are also comfortable *receiving* the critiques and feedback from the editor.

When this type of relationship is established, the manuscript/document has an even greater chance of being successful because the team behind the scenes was on one accord! As YWT client, Jessica Chattopadhyay stated, the editing process "went so smooth... She fixed every mistake... she went back many times to make sure [the book] was perfect for the readers as well as me, the new author." My goal as an editor is to capture Jessica's vision while fine-tuning her thoughts.

Lastly, a "good" editor will be very up front with the writer at all times. They will provide an NDA (non-disclosure agreement) or confidentiality agreement, for both parties to sign. This lets the writer know that the editor fully understands and agrees that the manuscript/ document they are being given access to is treated as highly personal, private and will be treated very precious and with the highest regard. It is very important to know that the writer trusts their editor completely and the editor does not take the writer's trust for granted. Once these boundaries are put in place, most editors and writers develop long-lasting literary relationships for future projects and providing referrals as well.

Editing Styles 101

Editing usually is, and is most effective, when done in "rounds." That means working on larger things first, then focusing on smaller things such as grammar, punctuation, and/or anything the writer would like focused on.

Round #1 will allow the editor to read the whole manuscript/document and provide feedback on the "whole," being able to advise if structural and flow/consistency or relevancy types of changes need to be made. When the writer finishes reviewing the first set of edits, round #2 begins and the editor will review the changes made by the writer, assess, then provide additional feedback and suggestions. Editor gives back to the writer; writer reviews and sends back to the editor.

These rounds continue until both the editor and writer are in agreement that no more changes need to be made and the manuscript/ document is ready for print.

There are various editing styles that are used when reading over a manuscript/ document. Just so we're on the same page – a manuscript is the technical, or official, name of a novel or book. Document refers to anything that someone wants edited that is not a novel or book. It can be a resume, article for a blog or magazine, paper for school or project, etc.

When editing, it is common that most writers don't know there is even a difference in editing styles. They just want the periods and commas fixed and of course catch those misspelled words. And if some words don't sound right or that sentence "don't flow right," take it out. LOL That's the truth! However, there are technical editing names for some of the styles and they make a difference in what the editor focuses on and how they rate their services. As you read through the editing styles below, it may seem that they are all the same but they aren't. The ones we discuss are the most commonly used. There are other editing styles that an editor may use as well. When you are researching potential editors, you can ask about the styles they use or what you need.

Yes, there are similarities, and they may overlap in the things that are focused on, however, each has its own role that is different from the other. This is why it is important for you to know the difference and be able to talk with your editor (or potential editor) about your concerns. **#doyourResearch**

Developmental Editing – this type of editing focuses on the manuscript/document as a whole, and it's usually the first step of editing once the content is complete. It's also the most intense and detailed type of editing.

The editor is going to look at the overall story/content and evaluate based on consistency, flow, and things like that. They will look at the plot/idea/theme structure and they may suggest if chapters need to be rearranged, deleted; if something needs to be expanded on or condensed. This type of editing may even suggest that the entire book should be rewritten. This style of editing is to look at the "bigger picture" and to help the writer be sure they have remained focused on their idea/theme and they are being as impactful as possible with their words and ideas.

Copy Editing - this is the style just about everyone asks for and they don't even know it's a style! (LOL) Copy editing focuses on spelling, punctuation, grammar, capitalization and basic writing mishaps. This can also be referred to as "mechanical" editing as it is looking at the mechanical and technical parts of the writing piece. There is also a focus on confirming if the writer wants to use 1st or 3rd person in their tone; or if they want to use passive or active voice. There is also a focus on if the wording used and overall writing quality is written to target the desired audience. The purpose is to provide that "fine tuning" and polish to the writer's manuscript/document.

Line Editing - it is a close relative of "copy" editing, however, there are some differences. Yes, line editing is exactly what it says: editing that is done line by line. Literally. Yes, attention is given to proofreading and grammar and things like that, but word choice is examined and the impact of those words to be sure those are the best choice for the book and how readers will react and relate. Line editing focuses on run-on sentences or phrases that may sound "over-used" or cliche.

An example of line editing would be:

UNEDITED –

The kids in the classroom were talking so loudly, I couldn't hear the teacher and their voices sounded like cackling hens. As I waited for them to stop and hopefully, they got in trouble, I doodled in my notebook. The teacher cleared her throat standing next to my desk, bringing my attention back to the classroom.

"I'm sorry. I didn't hear you. Can you repeat that?" I asked.

EDITED –

The classroom buzzed with noisy conversation from the students.

The teacher cleared her throat.

"I'm sorry. Can you repeat that?" I asked.

This is a "line" edit because none of the action or idea was changed, but what was changed was the words. They were cleaned up to be more concise and effective based on the scene.

Notes...

There is a cost: Editing Rates

Right next to "Do I need an editor?" is their sibling, "How much is this gonna cost?" I hate to burst your budgeting bubble, but yes, editing costs. It is part of the investment you will make in writing a successful book. And the rates vary. No, there's no "fixed" rate but I will tell you this: Always, Always, Always – do your research **FIRST**! I cannot stress that enough.

The worst thing you can do is hire an editor that may have quoted one thing, then doesn't stick to that rate. Or the type of editing you requested is not what they provided. Or the biggest thing that I have heard from clients and colleagues – you did not get anything in writing. Why (or how) did this happen? You agreed to work with this editor based on a verbal conversation over the phone, and the editor did not provide any written agreement to the rate, time frame for editing turnaround, how many revisions are included in the rate, and any other requirements necessary to complete the job.

When you are talking with editors and requesting rates, be sure they are very clear with their rate structure and do not be afraid to ask questions. The ones I'm going to mention are the two most common and the terms you will hear most often.

Per word - some editors will base their rates on a "per word" basis. This means you will need to provide them with the total word count of your manuscript/document to calculate the rate. Many authors like this type of rate because it allows them to know up front what they are looking at for cost. As always, if you want to work with an editor, let them know your budget and they may be flexible and willing to work with you. Some may offer payment plans which may allow you to pay a portion up front and the remainder upon completion.

How do you find the total word count?

If you are in MS (Microsoft) Word, at the top of your task bar, you can click on REVIEW and "Word Count" is one of the choices. Click that option & you will be given all of the "statistics:" total pages, words, characters with and without spaces, paragraphs & lines. You want to look at WORDS.

If you are in Google Docs, click on TOOLS in the task bar and look for "Word Count." You will use the controls - CTRL+SHIFT+C to get your word count. For other apps you may use, refer to their tool/task bar or Help section to find the word count.

For example: if you have 27,563 words and the editor's rate is $0.005/word for basic copyediting (grammar, proofreading, spelling, paragraph structure, etc.) you are looking at approximately $138 to edit. Not too bad, right? Yes, that rate is correct. It is $0.005 and not $0.05 because 0.005 is half a cent compared to 5 cents. When you are working with large documents that are more than 15-20,000 words it can become very costly. Whenever you receive a rate such as 0.005-0.009 it is less than 1 cent per word and those are pretty budget friendly. Again, do your research and confirm the rate from the editor.

There are also "tiered rates" in which editors may charge one rate for a certain amount of words. For example:

- Up to 2,000 words: $95 flat rate
- 2,000–3,999 words: $120 flat rate
- 4,000–5,999 words: $125 flat rate
- 6,000–39,999 words: $25 per 1,000 words

(NOTE: these are sample rates for demonstration purposes only)

Per page: The current market rate is approximately $3-4/page for basic copyediting. Again, this is an average, or general, rate. Depending on the editor and the type of editing you need, this price can vary. Per page may work better for you depending on the length of your document/manuscript. If you have something short, like, less than 12,000 words this may be the better rate for you. Or a tiered rate could work.

Again, do your research and talk with the editor you are considering working with. Let them know your budget, the length of your document & what type of editing you are looking for. That will make a huge difference. Also, please please keep this in mind: ***Do NOT sign any agreements or contracts until you have the rate and payment in writing and both of you agree to all the terms.***

Some editors charge a **minimum** fee for their services to cover the cost of their time and energy spent on a particular project in lieu of other services they may provide. Many editors also work in academics or hold advanced degrees, and their fee reflects the value of their time and their expertise. **#doyourResearch**

<u>PLEASE NOTE!</u> While researching, pay attention to market value rates to help you compare and make your decision. ***<u>Rates change!</u>***

If you hire a professional editor, the **average** cost is about $400 for a non-fiction book at approximately 20,000 words (that's about 40 pgs). That is a rate of about $0.02 per word. These rates are based on the type of editing you desire, which is why it is so important to talk with the editor you are interested in working with so they can discuss the *various* editing styles that will best fit your needs. Fiction books compared to non-fiction books may cost more. Developmental or structural editing costs more than copy editing, so please confirm the type of editing you would like.

It's all about research, folks. *<u>Research, research, research.</u>* The more you educate yourself, the more you will be able to protect yourself and have the tools you need to successfully complete your book project. As always, the YWT staff is ready and available to answer any questions you may have. Contact us today!

Preparing Your Manuscript

Once you have hired an editor, there are still a few more steps to getting your book ready for print and publish. Not only does the editor have to read through your book from start to finish, but they have to also get it ready for printing. There are certain rules and guidelines that printers/publishers require in order to successfully and correctly print your book. Whether it's an e-book or print book, editing is the last – and most critical- step that you need to pay attention to.

Most of the time books are written (or typed) on a standard sheet of paper which is 8.5" x 11". Most paperback books are smaller than that, and they are reduced to 6"x9". The literary world calls this "trade paperback" size. When the editor is done reading through your book, they will "format" the book into the size you want for printing. 6x9 is the most common, however, books can be printed larger or smaller if desired. You can discuss that with your editor. If you aren't sure of what size your printed book should be, look at other books in your genre to help you make the decision. (Your editor can also assist you as well.)

Here's a *Winning Writing* Tip! When working with your manuscript in Google Docs or another platform, the layout/way it looks will NOT look the same when it is converted to a Microsoft Word document. Google Docs is GREAT for editing and working in real-time with your editor because of the notes/comment box and both of you can access the document at the same time and see each other's keystrokes on the screen.

When it is time for the book to be printed, most on-demand printers and even local, brick & mortar printers want the manuscript in PDF format which means everything – all edits and content – must be done and ready to go by the time it gets to the printer. When the editor tells you it may take a couple weeks to format and layout your book, they are repositioning paragraphs and ensuring all your content converted correctly.

The next part in getting your book ready for print is the layout. Layout is putting the "meat" of the book – the content together. That includes putting page numbers in position (top or bottom of the page, center or left/right-hand side), headers and any other things you want at the top of the page in your desired position.

Layout is also what type of font/typeface you want, the size of the font, the style, and all that good stuff. You also decide what position you want your page numbers in: bottom center of the page, left or right-hand corner or upper left or right-hand corner. Do you want just the number or do you want it to say "Page 1" or something else?

This is when you will talk with your editor or design team and let them know what your ideas are. They can also give you suggestions on the best type of font size and style based on your content and book cover ideas.

In addition to font and page numbering, laying out your book also includes the headers, or as some people call them, "the running titles" at the top of the pages. The headers are usually the author name and the book title. They can be in the center of the page or on the left/right-hand corners. You can look at the top of these pages for an example. Headers are not mandatory, however, they do add some pizazz and sparkle to your book.

Lastly, don't forget about your other pages such as Table of Contents, Acknowledgements, Preface, Prologue, Dedication, Foreword, and of course About the Author. Acknowledgements and Foreword are not mandatory either, however, they are included in many non-fiction books. Fiction books include these, too, but not the Foreword so much.

The purpose of the Foreword is to have someone introduce the book the readers and give credibility to the author and/or book. Basically, that person is gonna "vouch" for you and say your book is the bomb, you are the bomb and they support you! (LOL)

The Preface is not really necessary, but it is used in fiction and non-fiction books. The purpose of the Preface is to give a brief, introductory summary which explains the author's reason for writing the book/telling the story. This is also where the author would share what they hope the reader will learn from the book.

Prologues are a little different from the Preface in that the Prologue is used more in fiction books. It is the starting point of the story and provides the background and set-up. It basically gives the reader a little behind the scenes and heads up on what to expect from the book without giving away the plot or storyline.

Your editor will go over all these things with you to be sure you want or need to include them; and also discuss why you may or may not need those sections. Be sure that you talk with them about all your ideas. It's the only way they will know what you are thinking about and how you would like your manuscript prepared.

Quick Editing Checklist

Here is a recap of what we reviewed in this section and you can use it for all your writing projects so you don't forget what to look for when deciding to hire an editor.

When you are getting ready to select an editor, be sure to **DO YOUR RESEARCH** & use the following before making your selection:

- ✓ Review your manuscript & decide what type of editing you need (developmental, copy, line, etc.)
- ✓ Did the editor discuss the editing styles with you?
- ✓ What is your budget?
- ✓ Are payment plans available if you need one?
- ✓ What are their forms of payment?
- ✓ Does the editor have any samples of their work for you to see their work or will they provide a sample edit for you?
- ✓ Was the editor easy to talk to/were they able to understand your vision for your manuscript/document?
- ✓ What is their turnaround time?

- ✓ Does the editor provide a written agreement stating what services they will provide & the final rate?
- ✓ Does the editor have a website or references for you to research & gain more knowledge about them?

Notes...

Notes...

Part III:
Winning at PUBLISHING and PROMOTING

Self-pub vs Traditional pub

Years ago, traditional publishing was the ONLY way to get your book published. Self-publishing has actually been around since the 1800's. There's a whole lotta history and facts on how it really started, and I shall not bore you with those details in this book. I will say that Charles Dickens, you know, the one who wrote "A Christmas Carol?" He self-published that book in 1872 and sold out of his first print run of 6,000 copies. Isn't that crazy? Yes, this is the same book that Disney turned into an animated movie where Donald Duck played Scrooge. It has also been redone many times on the big screen and in countless school and theatre plays.

I digress. But you get the point of how ONE self-published book took off and the impact it had.

Today, due to platforms like Amazon/KDP, Lulu, Ingram Sparks and others, it is much easier to publish your book on your own. There are pros and cons, of course, when choosing self-publishing so as we have said many times in this book, do your research! See what works best for YOU and go with that. Don't ever feel pressured to do something because another author did it a particular way. Your book is your book, and you have to stay focused on *your* goals and *your* vision.

Self-publishing is when a writer owns the rights and all royalties (sales) from their book; and they are not connected to or contracted with a "traditional" publishing company such as Bantam, Random House Books, or Simon & Schuster. The writer also has full creative control over their book from cover to content, and complete control over marketing. Self-published books also tend to have a higher profit margin compared to traditionally published books, and your books can hit the market within a shorter time frame than traditionally published books.

Self-publishing is perfect for the first-time author, entrepreneur, lawyers, doctors, financial planners, business executives, and those who "just wanna write a book." Self-publishing is also the best way to go if you want TOTAL creative control over your content and ideas; and if you want TOTAL freedom with no one telling you how to write and what to write about. There is also long-term wealth that comes with being a self-published author because you are able to continue marketing and selling your book on YOUR terms with no pressure on how many books "must" be sold within a particular amount of time. In addition, you are able to make an impact being self-published because you can choose to write on a "niche" topic such as the type of business you are in and target your marketing towards those in that same industry/field. Your following will be able to grow due to your book and the value you are providing.

On the downside to self-publishing, there are investments that have to be made out of pocket for marketing, hiring an editor and/or graphic designer, and you have to put in the time to learn and manage the publishing process. Basically, everything is on YOU... however, there are book-writing consultants/ coaches (such as ***Your Writing Table***) who provide all these services to assist you with the process. Yes, there are still fees to have these services done, however, consulting/coaching agencies like these are in business to help writers get their book published and they still hold all rights and royalties.

Traditional publishing means the company owns the print license for the book, but the writer/author DOES own the copyright to their book. The only way the publishing company will have access to the copyright of your book will be if you literally "assign it" to them. Assigning the copyright means the traditional publisher transfers ALL rights of your book to the publisher and you lose ALL control of your book. It belongs to the publishing company. **DO NOT DO EVER DO THIS!!!** Authors want to always, always keep and control the copyright for your book. It's *your* work!

The publishing company also controls the royalties and sales, which is usually 15% for hardcover and about 8% for paperback. The profit margin is very low, but when the high number of sales come through, that is what makes the difference. The **volume** of books sold is what increases the profit.

It is very difficult to get an offer to be published through a traditional book company. Unfortunately, an extremely small percentage of all manuscript proposals are accepted by traditional publishers. They are looking for specific types of books and certain types of clients. Rejection letters from traditional publishers can be very discouraging and it can cause some writers to give up and decide to stop pursuing their dream of becoming published.

Guess what??? It's okay! I want you to push through and keep going. If you have submitted a proposal to a traditional publisher and they rejected you, it's okay!!! Your work is still awesome! Don't quit!!

Sometimes writers hire a literary agent to represent them to pitch the book idea to traditional publishers. An agent's job is to review your manuscript and present it to various publishers hoping they will be interested and offer a book deal. Some of the most popular traditional publishers located in New York won't even look at a manuscript if it is not presented by a literary agent, but if your book is accepted, you could get a very lucrative book deal. If you are interested in hiring with a literary, do your research! Be sure that they are going to do what you need them to and be sure to confirm their fees.

A large number of the people who are offered publishing deals are major celebrities, athletes, politicians, musicians, A-list actors/actresses, or professional writers who have a long history of high-volume sales. If the company likes the idea a publishing deal is offered, and the author has to agree to turn over ALL the rights of their book in exchange for a cash advance on the royalties. If a cash advance is offered, it is usually in the 6-figure range and it is based on the number of "expected" or anticipated book sales. (Side note: cash advances do NOT have to be paid back to the publishing company so even if the book does not sell what was anticipated, that money stays with the writer. Period.) The publishing company buys the license to print the book, then they take over the whole publishing and book distribution process.

One major downside with traditional publishers is that the print license belongs to them, so you are not able to or allowed to print your book anywhere. In addition, you LOSE all creative control.

As they own the license, that means they own all the content – word for word – you do not have the final say in what the book cover will look like, what words will be removed or changed or chapters deleted, etc. They even get to decide what is included in your author bio.

Contrary to popular belief, publishing companies do not handle any marketing. They leave that up to the author. Their goal is to have the author do all the selling and promotion of the book. This is why celebrities, athletes and other influencers have lots of sales – they already have a huge audience/following.

For example, Tabitha Brown, who is a huge social media influencer has over 4 million followers on Instagram, over 3 million followers on Facebook, a TV show on the Food Network, many endorsements with seasoning/spice companies and other businesses, so she is what can be considered a "household name." Many many people know who Tabitha Brown is. She recently debuted a clothing line in Target stores and when she promoted her seasoning on social media, she sold out in minutes. It was no surprise that her book sales for her book, "Feeding the Soul," was a #1 New York Times Bestseller and top seller on Amazon and other platforms. She has a gigantic fan-base and audience who loves her. Not only does she have the benefit of mainstream media attention, but she also has the budget to pay for top quality PR (public relations) and media folks to get out there and market her name. Her name is a "brand" in itself, which adds to the value of her book. (That is a totally separate topic, but yep, that plays a part, too!)

Marketing & Promotion

As we discussed in the previous section, marketing and promotion is on you - the author. Even with a traditional publisher, as we learned, YOU have to be the one to spread the word and let the world know you have a book for them to purchase. You have some value and knowledge you want to share; you have a story that has some outstanding characters they must become familiar with. You have to become creative on how to market and promote.

Selling your book actually starts **before** you write it, in all honesty. You can begin introducing characters and book ideas/themes while you are creating the content. Social media is one of the best (and FREE) ways to do this. Post teasers and snippets of the book on your page, reels/stories frequently and begin to create a buzz. Your current followers who are already familiar with you and your written work will be ready to purchase. Those who are just getting to know you, new followers, or if you are on a new social media platform, will begin to learn more about you and the book as you continue to share your posts. Also, be sure to engage and interact with your followers. If they comment or ask a question, respond so they know you are just as interested in their thoughts. It also lets them know you appreciate them caring about what you post.

One way to create your posts is not to just write text but add an image/picture of the book cover once it's ready. You can hire a graphic designer to create images for you or you can use FREE tools such as Canva (www.canva.com) to create posts for Instagram, Facebook & other social media platforms. You can also create reels and stories that will also help to draw attention. (Instagram & TikTok are BIG when it comes to reels & stories. If you are not familiar with them or how to set them up, YouTube "University" always has tutorials available that you can watch for free.) I have used Canva many times along with the help of professional graphic designers. Research what will work best for you and go with it! Your goal is to share, share, and gain more exposure to pick up followers who will be interested in buying your book.

The more you post and share, the more your book will be seen by not only your followers, but they may share the post with others and that's even greater exposure. You can also use paid advertising which will allow you to expand the reach of your post. Facebook and IG are great examples of how paid advertising can really increase your exposure. You can set your budget for as little as $2 or $3 per day for a period of days. You also set the demographics (location, male/female, age range, etc.) and let the ads do the rest!

I used this method a few times for a conference/ workshop I was hosting a few years ago and it was successful. I was able to connect with those who I wasn't friends with on social media and they attended the conference based on the post that was shared. Yes, this totally works for not just sharing pictures of your book but also events that you are having. Speaking engagements and book signings, live events, vendor pop-ups and more. The goal is to spread the word as much as possible.

NOTE: Canva is also an excellent tool for any type of advertising and marketing that you would like to use for promotion. You can create newsletters, magazines, flyers, even business cards on this amazing website. It is FREE to sign up and there is an option to upgrade and receive access to more graphics, designs and other perks.

Also, KNOW your stuff! What do I mean? If it's a fictional book, KNOW the storyline! KNOW the characters as if they are real live people who live in your neighborhood or your classmates from school. The more excitement you bring, it will also get your followers excited, too! Do a few live streams to talk about one or two characters and to build anticipation for the book.

If it's a non-fiction/self-help (or other categories) KNOW your content as well. Position yourself as an expert in your field/area of study and let potential readers/customers know what type of value they will receive as a result of reading your book and/or working with you. The more personal experience you provide along with statistics and factual information, it will show your readers .

As you do this, followers WILL spread the word and they will share your posts. It may "seem" like people aren't reading books but here's a lil' secret — reading is STILL a huge industry. Yes, people love to read a good book whether it's digital or print. There is still a very big interest in print books and the fact that self-publishing is an option is continuing to add to the population of published authors.

This is a sidebar, but it fits perfectly with this conversation! LOL I'm just gonna drop this lil nugget so you guys can get an even better understanding of how strong this book game really is!

When the COVID-19 pandemic hit in March 2020 and the world was pretty much on shutdown, people were home and began to really explore the idea of becoming published authors. Many people had been thinking of writing a book for years and being stuck in the house gave them the discipline they needed to go on and finish the idea they started. There were so many people who decided to accomplish their goal of becoming a published author, it became a "trend." Writing a book was something people wanted to do more and more because they had time on their hands. As more people decided to write, online publish &

print platforms, or "print on demand" companies such as Amazon and Lulu.com saw huge increases of books and journals being published.

As a matter of fact, within the last five years, self-publishing has increased more than 250%! And here is another interesting fact: more than 65% of the top-rated self-published books are written by **women**! So, you are not alone in the "ocean" of books that are self-published just about every day. This is why marketing/advertising and promotion are so important. Your book is literally one among millions of books. How can yours stand out??

Exposure is the name of the game. If people don't know you have a book for sale, they won't be able to buy it, right? Get yourself out there! And if you're shy, don't really like talking in front of crowds or being on a live stream, that is going to present a challenge because you have to be able to reach out and "sell" your book! Here are some ideas for getting exposure:

- ✓ Book Fairs
- ✓ Vendor pop-up shops
- ✓ Book signings/launch party

- ✓ Website/landing page
- ✓ Networking/connecting with others who can help promote your book
- ✓ Social media live streams/reels/stories
- ✓ Paid ads for magazines, newspapers & social media
- ✓ Podcasts (we have one you can be a guest on, too! See the end of the book for info!)

You can also market and promote your book through your email database. If you don't have an email list, you should start working on that, like, yesterday. Having an email list will allow you to connect to your followers/fans by providing incentives such as a discount on early bird purchases of your book or even giving them an earlier time slot to pre-order the book. You can build your email list many ways as well.

One way is to offer a sneak peek of a part of the new book. You can create a post on social media telling them you are going to share a chapter of the book, but they have to sign up in order to receive it. Or you can offer a gift/giveaway in exchange for email sign up. For example, you can say you are doing a contest and the prize is a $10 gift card for all those who sign up for the email list. A drawing will be done, and the winner will be notified. (The prize doesn't have to be a gift card… it can be anything you choose. It's all about the "free" thing that is being offered which attracts people.)

If you prefer not to do any marketing or promotion on your own, you can definitely hire a virtual assistant or someone skilled in this area to do this for you. They specialize in this and they know the tips and tools on how to get you the greatest exposure. I know how it is trying to learn all this technology and social media do's and don'ts. It can get really confusing and frustrating if you don't have the time to put into learning how it all works AND keeping up with the changes. I have worked with a couple of these social media geniuses and they continue to blow my mind! I just shared my ideas and goals, and they did the rest. The results were much better than anything I ever could have come up with! (HA HA)

As always, do your research and be sure to ask questions before agreeing to a contract. Be sure they are going to provide exactly what you are looking for and they understand your goals for your book.

Lastly, podcasts have become more popular now than every before. Whether it's audio or video, being a guest on a podcast is a really great way to gain exposure and promote your book. Audio podcasts have their episodes on platforms such as iHeart Radio, Amazon Music, Spotify, and Apple Podcasts. Most people can access these platforms on their smartphones or tablets/computers. Video podcasts are usually on YouTube where the podcast producer will create a YouTube channel to post all of the episodes and content. Videos are also done on Instagram and Facebook through Livestreams or they're pre-recorded then posted.

Research the particular show you would like to be a guest on and contact the host/producer and ask what the requirements are to be featured on their show. This is the same if you are invited to be a guest… be sure to ask any/all questions before you agree to be on the show.

YWT has a podcast – *Women Winning at Writing* which is a platform for women writers to talk about their books, their book writing journey and more! We talk with women who are first-time writers, seasoned writers and those who are in the process of writing their book. The conversations are enlightening, entertaining and an awesome way for the writers to get exposure that they didn't have before. Many of the guests have had increased book sales and increases in followers on social media as a result of being on the show.

(If you would like to be a guest or you know someone who may be interested, go to the end of the book for more info!)

In Closing...

Hopefully, this wasn't too boring! You made it to the end or you skipped through to the sections that pertained to you, but either way, you are reading this last and final chapter, so...

CONGRATULATIONS!

My hope is that now that you have reached this point, you have learned a lil' sumthin sumthin on how to **WIN** at writing and editing. This book does not provide ALL of the ways to win at writing and editing... no way! This is definitely a select *few* of the tips and tools that are used regularly by *Your Writing Table*. All of our clients have been successful when implementing these tips, tools, and strategies and we encourage you to do the same.

In order to win at writing... and editing, you must be dedicated, driven, determined and have one of those "I refuse to quit" mindsets. This will allow you to not only complete creating your content but to also be successful with editing, and marketing and promoting your book. It may seem impossible, but writing a book is not as hard as it has been made out to be. I would say that depending on the genre/topic of your book can determine the level of complexity with writing it. I can also say that once you get an idea and you feel the inspiration hit, you'll be able to write more than you think! I had a client who wrote his book in less than one week. A colleague of mine wrote her in book about two weeks after she created her outline. When the inspiration hits, go with it and allow the ideas to flow. You'll be so glad you did!

As it has been said throughout the book, DO YOUR RESEARCH and DO YOUR RESEARCH. Your book is *your* vision and *your* dream, so it is important for you to be sure that everything you do from hiring a coach, an editor and/or social media manager to assist with the book-writing process are the people you are comfortable with. Be sure their rates fit with your budget and your communication with them is open and smooth.

Writing your book is an investment not only for legacy that your family and loved ones will be able to hold on to forever, but it is also an investment in **YOU**.

You are taking the time to document ideas, knowledge, facts, and memories that you want to leave with your loved ones. You are also providing value and education for those who are doing the same thing you are within business or any area.

Your Writing Table congratulates you for making the decision to write a book. Whether it's your first or your fifth, we are proud of you for sharing your literary gifts with the world. If our team can assist you in any way, please don't hesitate to contact us.

ONE LAST THING...

Before you go, I would like for you to do a couple things. It's free and won't take long! Thank you so much & I appreciate you!

Share this book with others who are thinking about writing a book or need editing services. **Share** the posts on social media and most important – please leave a review on Amazon.com

If you aren't following me on social media, please do so:

Facebook: YourWriting Table

Instagram: @coach_chelsiamccoy

Notes...

Notes...

Notes...

References & Recommended Sources

Pg. 48: Plottr
https://plottr.com/?utm_source=blog&utm_medium=guest%20po
st&utm_campaign=Camp%20NaNoWriMo%202021

pg.49: NaNoWriMo
https://blog.nanowrimo.org/post/6587896767765806592/4-easy-
steps-for-outlining-a-novel-as-a-pantser

pg. 56
Scherstuhl, A. (2022). "Just Do It (Yourself): A History of Self-
Publishing. Publisher's Weekly. Retrieved from:
https://www.publishersweekly.com/pw/by-topic/industry-
news/publisher-news/article/88987-just-do-it-yourself-a-history-
of-self-publishing.html

Pg.62
Max, T. (2023). "Self-Publishing vs Traditional in 2023. (Which is
Better?) Retrieved from: https://scribemedia.com/self-publishing-
vs-
traditional/#:~:text=What%20Is%20the%20Difference%20Between,
the%20book%20is%20traditionally%20published

pg. 119
Rizzo, N. "Self-published Books & Authors Sales Statistics
[2023]". (2022.) Retrieved from: https://wordsrated.com/self-
published-book-sales-statistics/

About the Author

Chelsia McCoy has been reading since she was a little girl, and she wrote her first full-length novel in junior high school. For over 20 years, she has not only written her own books, but she has been helping others write their books or assist them with editing and other types of writing projects. Her love of writing and the written word comes from within and as she often tells people, it's in her DNA! She loved it so much she went to school and now holds a Master's degree in Communication!

She's a California-born-then-turned Houstonian who's a mom of 3 and dog-mom to a spoiled Chi-Weenie! So, she's a Cali-Texan or a Texa-fornian, right? Or somethin' like that. Either way, she's sippin' on sweet tea, eatin' some good Mexican cuisine while fulfilling clients' writing & editing dreams.

In addition to working on her own books, she is the founder and CEO of *Your Writing Table*, a full-service consulting agency providing book-writing, formatting, editing, publishing, ghostwriting, & audio and video transcription services. She is also the creator and founder of the podcast show, *Women Winning at Writing*, which talks about all things writing & editing from a woman's perspective. The show provides a platform for women to talk about their writing &

editing journeys while breaking down the myths of book-writing and editing.

She is also an 8x-Amazon best-selling editor, and co-executive producer of the Amazon Prime Video documentary she also stars in titled, "*When the Soul Cries: Trauma Tears, Triumph,*" which is a collaborative anthology.

Her goal is to inspire and remind you that each of us has a story to tell.

Her motto: Don't wait for someone to invite you to their table. **Create *your* own table and tell *your* story *your* way, in *your* words!**

More books by Chelsia McCoy:

Only 'Cause You're My Brother: A Novel

Hand On the Closet: Hope & Healing in Relationships

Say It Right: 5 Tools for Effective Communication

When the Soul Cries: Trauma, Tears, Triumph

Coming Soon: This Faith Walk!
(look for it --Summer 2024)

We would love to hear from you!

Follow Chelsia on social media:

Facebook: YourWritingTable
Instagram: @coach_chelsiamccoy
LinkedIn: @CoachChelsiaMcCoy

To get updates on the podcast:
Instagram: @womenwinningatwritingpodcast

Attention all women writers!

We are excited about our new platform
where we talk about ALL
things writing & editing!
If you would like to be a guest on our
show, access the link below to schedule
a call! We would love to talk with you!

To book a Podcast Show Consultation:
https://calendly.com/ywtconsult
You can also send an email:
support@yourwritingtable.com
for all inquiries or concerns!

Interested in writing your own book?
Have you written your book and now
you need editing services?
You have an "idea" for a book,
but you need some guidance
on what to do next?
You recorded some content on Zoom or on
an audio recording and now you would like it
converted to written format?
WE CAN HELP YOU!

Visit our website:
www.yourwritingtable.com
Or send us an email:
support@yourwritingtable.com
You can also call or text! (832) 334-2706